Just the Facts

Depression

Claire Wallerstein

Heinemann Library
Chicago, Illinois

Customer Service 888-454-2279
Visit our website at www.heinemannlibrary.com

Designed by Jane Hawkins
Originated by Ambassador Litho Ltd.
Printed and bound in China by South China Printing Company

07 06 05 04 03
10 9 8 7 6 5 4 3 2 1

Library of Congress Cataloging-in-Publication Data
Wallerstein, Claire, 1969-
  Depression / Claire Wallerstein.
     p. cm. -- (Just the facts)
Summary: Explains what depression is, offers a look at depression
throughout history, and describes what causes people to get depressed,
why depression is increasing among young people, and various treatment
options.
Includes bibliographical references and index.
  ISBN 1-4034-0818-1
  1. Depression, Mental--Juvenile literature. [1. Depression, Mental.]
I. Title. II. Series.
  RC537 .W355 2003
  616.85'27--dc21

                                    2002010937

Acknowledgments
The author and publisher are grateful to the following for permission to reproduce copyright material:
Cover photograph: Cameron/Corbis Stock Market.
p. 4 Jim Varney/Science Photo Library; p. 5 Paul Baldesare/Photofusion; p. 7 Andrew Testa/Rex Features; p. 8 Image Works/Topham Picturepoint; p. 9 Popperfoto; pp. 10, 42 Topham Picturepoint; p. 11 Erich Lessing/AKG London; p. 12 Berry Bingel/Rex Features; p. 13 Kevin Fleming/Corbis; p. 15 Sean Sprague/Still Pictures; p. 17 Popperfoto; p. 18 Facelly/Rex Features; p. 19 Ron Giling/Still Pictures; p. 20 Popperfoto; p. 22 Alfred Pasieka/Science Photo Library; p. 23 S. Cinti, CNRI/Science Photo Library; p. 25 Camera Press; p. 26 Fotos International/Rex Features; p. 27 AKG London; p. 28 Charles Gupton/Corbis Stock Market; p. 29 Ute Klaphake/Photofusion; p. 30 Shawn Baldwin/Associated Press; p. 32 Paul Doyle/ Photofusion; p. 33 L. Willatt, East Anglian Regional Genetics Service/Science Photo Library; p. 34 Rex Features; p. 35 Mauro Fermariello/Science Photo Library; p. 37 Christa Stadtler/Photofusion; p. 38 Paul Baldesare/Photofusion; p. 39 Geoff Tompkinson/Science Photo Library; p. 40 John Birdsall Photography; p. 44 CC Studio/Science Photo Library; p. 45 Paul Baldesare/Photofusion; p. 47 John Griem/Science Photo Library; p. 48 Jim Wvinner/Science Photo Library; p. 50 W. Schmitz/Bilderberg/Network Photographers.

Every effort has been made to contact copyright holders of any material reproduced in this book. Any omissions will be rectified in subsequent printings if notice is given to the publisher.

Our special thanks to Pamela G. Richards, M.Ed., for her help in the preparation of the book.

Some words appear in bold, **like this.** You can find out what they mean by looking in the glossary.

Contents

Depression

Marilyn Monroe, one of the most glamorous movie idols of all time, seemed to have it all—fame, beauty, money, and a string of handsome husbands and boyfriends. However, she suffered from one of the world's most common illnesses—depression. By the early 1960s, Monroe was under the almost constant care of a **psychiatrist.** She was also taking huge amounts of drugs to fight off the feelings of gloom, despair, and low self-esteem that tormented her. In 1962 she committed **suicide** at the age of 36.

A common condition

Experts say that up to one-third of people will suffer from depression at some point in their lives. Women are affected twice as often as men. One person in twenty is depressed at any one time. It is not only adults who suffer from this illness. Young people get depressed, too. In fact, with each generation, depression now seems to hit more people, and at a younger age. The reasons for this are not fully understood.

For people who have never suffered from depression, the condition can be very hard to understand. Depression can make people lose the will and energy to do even simple things, such as getting out of bed. Depressed people are more likely than the general population to get sick, have accidents, and not eat or sleep properly. In severe cases, they are also more likely to take their own lives.

Depression is already the cause of almost 30 percent of all days taken off work. Experts at the World Health Organization (WHO) predict that depression will be the world's second-leading root cause of death by 2020. Despite this, it is thought that doctors may fail to diagnose up to half of all cases of depression. Many people are too embarrassed to talk about their problems or seek treatment. Instead, they may suffer in silence for years. This is unfortunate, because in most cases depression can be treated.

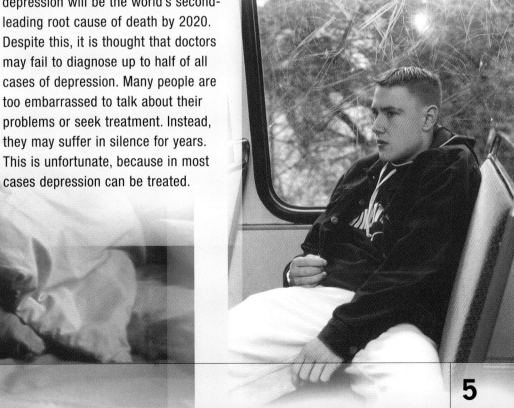

"I looked around me at the other people on the bus. I couldn't understand how the older ones could possibly have got to the age they had, as life was so terrible. Every day was an ordeal."

(Anonymous depression sufferer, quoted in the book *Depression* by Professor Edzard Ernst)

What Is Depression?

Depression is a very difficult condition to define. It is often referred to as the "common cold of **psychiatry"** because it seems to be so widespread. Even animals seem to get depressed in some situations.

The word *depression* does not just describe one illness, but various conditions, ranging from the natural sadness we feel, such as after a loved one dies, to major depression, which is usually caused by chemical imbalances in the brain.

How does it feel?

Many sufferers say that having depression is like living inside a gray fog or feeling numb all the time. Some depressed people may cry a lot, stop caring about how they look, and seem very tired. Others may put on a brave face, so the people around them have no idea that there is anything wrong.

People with what is called **manic depression** may sometimes seem like the most confident and lively people in the world—the "life of the party."

In one very unusual kind of depression, known as Cotard's **delusion,** sufferers are convinced they are actually dead and no longer have any organs inside their bodies. People with this condition may even try to kill themselves to prove to others that they are dead.

Diagnosing depression

Unlike more obvious illnesses such as the measles, which makes the patient break out in red spots, there is no easy way to diagnose depression. Doctors use a checklist of more than 50 symptoms, at least six of which must have been overwhelming for more than two weeks. Some of the most common symptoms include **insomnia** or sleeping too much, being unable to enjoy things that were once fun, overeating or losing weight, inability to make decisions, extreme loss of energy, feelings of guilt, and, in severe cases, frequent thoughts of death or **suicide.**

6

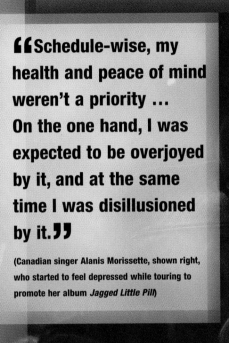

"Schedule-wise, my health and peace of mind weren't a priority …
On the one hand, I was expected to be overjoyed by it, and at the same time I was disillusioned by it."

(Canadian singer Alanis Morissette, shown right, who started to feel depressed while touring to promote her album *Jagged Little Pill*)

Types of depression

Until recently, **psychiatrists** believed that depression was either *endogenous* (coming from inside) or *reactive* (reacting to events in a person's life, such as unemployment, divorce, or stress). We now know that the causes of depression are more complicated than this. Since 1994, depression has been classified using a more accurate system called DSM4. DSM4 is a guide for doctors to help them diagnose mental disorders such as depression more accurately. Some of the main categories are major depressive disorder, **manic depression,** substance-induced **mood disorder,** and **dysthmia.**

Major depressive disorder (MDD)

Major depressive disorder (MDD) is also known as a mood disorder, or **affective disorder.** MDD is twice as common in women as it is in men. Without treatment, MDD lasts roughly nine months to a year. Some sufferers may not be able to continue to work or take care of themselves properly. In severe cases they may even become obsessed with thoughts of **suicide.**

Manic depression

Manic depression is a kind of MDD. However, when sufferers start to recover from the lows of depression, instead of returning to normal, they enter an episode of mania.

Stressful events, such as school exams, may spark a bout of depression.

People suffering from manic depression may be incredibly happy and energetic, or find it hard to calm down, be very easily irritated, and have signs of **psychosis.** Psychosis is a term used when someone suffers from **hallucinations** and **delusions.** Manic depression is a rare condition. It affects approximately one percent of the world's population. It is sometimes called **bipolar disorder** because of its two changing moods (*bi* means "two" in Latin). Depression alone is called **unipolar disorder** (*uni* means "one") because it just involves one mood—low and bleak.

Substance-induced mood disorder

Substance-induced mood disorder is depression brought on or made worse by using alcohol or drugs. These substances affect levels of important chemicals in the brain, especially if a person has been using them for a long time and has become **addicted.**

Dysthmia

The term *dysthmia* comes from the Greek word meaning "bad state of mind." The symptoms are similar to, but not as bad as, those of MDD. Sufferers can usually carry on with a fairly normal life, but the condition may last for at least two years.

Depression Throughout History

Depression has always existed. As long ago as 1600 B.C.E., the ancient Egyptians used plant remedies to treat people suffering from depression, or **melancholia.** Later, ancient Greek and Roman doctors recommended remedies such as poppy extract and donkey's milk, as well as gymnastics, massage, and baths.

By the Middle Ages in Europe, treatment for depression had become more barbaric. It was a common belief that depression sufferers and people with other mental illnesses were possessed by evil spirits. They were often tied up or locked away in prison-like **lunatic asylums.**

In the 19th century, there was a large increase in the number of people with depression. This was the time of the Industrial Revolution, when millions of people moved from the countryside to overcrowded, polluted cities. French **sociologist** Emile Durkheim blamed this breakdown in traditional lifestyles for the rise in stress, anxiety, and depression.

Depression can become more common during times when life is harder for everyone. In the 1930s, many people became depressed during a period of

In the past, many asylums for the mentally ill were violent and frightening places.

high unemployment and poverty known as the Great Depression. The word *depression* can refer to a downturn in the economy as well as in a person's state of mind.

Early treatments

The first **antidepressants** were not developed until the late 1950s. Until then, the only medicines available were drugs called pep pills. These could rapidly lift a person's mood. However, a short while later the person would crash into a severe depression. Pep pills were also **addictive.** Some desperate people resorted to drastic surgery, such as **lobotomies,** in the hope of a cure. In a lobotomy operation, surgeons separate the frontal lobes of the brain—the part responsible for a person's emotions—from the rest of the brain.

ʺThere is no happiness in life, only occasional flares of it.ʺ

(Leo Tolstoy, author of the epic novel *War and Peace*, who was a depression sufferer)

Famous sufferers

Many historical figures have suffered from depression, including Abraham Lincoln, who called his depression "the shadow of madness." Winston Churchill, the British prime minister during World War II, coined the phrase "black dog" to describe his own illness. Sigmund Freud, the inventor of **psychoanalysis,** who treated hundreds of depressed patients, was a sufferer, too.

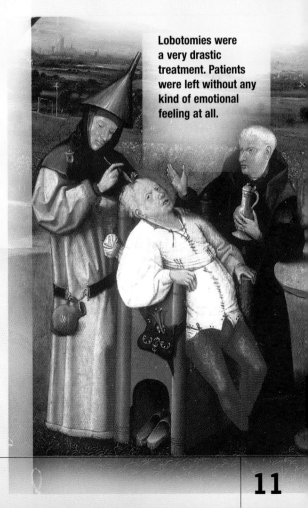

Lobotomies were a very drastic treatment. Patients were left without any kind of emotional feeling at all.

Who Suffers from Depression?

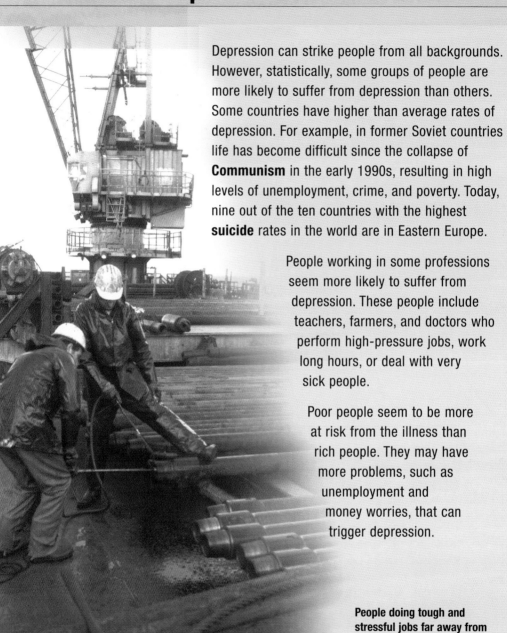

Depression can strike people from all backgrounds. However, statistically, some groups of people are more likely to suffer from depression than others. Some countries have higher than average rates of depression. For example, in former Soviet countries life has become difficult since the collapse of **Communism** in the early 1990s, resulting in high levels of unemployment, crime, and poverty. Today, nine out of the ten countries with the highest **suicide** rates in the world are in Eastern Europe.

People working in some professions seem more likely to suffer from depression. These people include teachers, farmers, and doctors who perform high-pressure jobs, work long hours, or deal with very sick people.

Poor people seem to be more at risk from the illness than rich people. They may have more problems, such as unemployment and money worries, that can trigger depression.

People doing tough and stressful jobs far away from home, such as these oil rig workers, may be at greater risk for depression.

Feeling isolated from society

People living in the countryside may suffer depression more than people living in cities. Poverty, lack of job opportunities, and feelings of isolation are often big problems in rural areas. In 2001, depression and suicide among British farmers rose dramatically when a huge outbreak of foot and mouth disease forced many of them to kill their animals.

Some studies have shown that people in ethnic minority groups may get depressed more than others, possibly because they feel cut off from their culture and home country. For example, Asian women living in the United States seem to be more at risk than white women. However, there are other factors, too. Many people from ethnic minorities are poorer and have more problems to deal with than the white majority.

High levels of unemployment and poverty, such as on this Navajo-Hopi Indian reservation, may be partly responsible for increasing depression among native societies.

Depression also seems less common among people with traditional hunting or farming lifestyles, who live in small, close-knit communities. Instances of depression among native people in the United States, Australia, and Canada used to be rare. Today, however, traditional lifestyles have mostly disappeared, and depression is rising faster in these groups than among the white population.

When can depression strike? Many doctors still mistakenly see depression as an adult disease. However, cases of depression among young people are on the increase. Children can sometimes suffer depression because of parents pressuring them to do well at school, or because of bullying, abuse, or problems with alcohol or drugs. Until their teens, boys are more likely than girls to suffer from depression. When they are older, females seem to get depressed roughly twice as often as males. These statistics may not show the whole picture, as boys are often more embarrassed than girls to admit how they feel. In a 2001 survey by the international support group Samaritans, about twenty percent of young people said they would laugh at a male friend if he said he was depressed. It is possible that boys' depression may be masked, coming out instead in violence, theft, drug-taking, or heavy drinking.

Depression seems to hit hardest among middle-aged people. These people may have to deal with problems such as job stress or divorce. They may feel there is nothing left to look forward to. Elderly people often become depressed, too. They may have to cope with the death of a husband or wife, sickness, pain, or the realization that they may no longer be able to look after themselves.

❝When he was four or five he would make comments like, 'The playground's a lonely place,' and, 'You'd be better off if I'd never been born.'❞

(Social worker Lindy Garnette, speaking on CNN about her depressed fourteen-year-old son Ben)

Depression in developing countries

Nearly all research into depression has been done in Western, industrialized countries. But 80 percent of the world's population lives, often in very difficult conditions, in **developing**

countries. Experts believe that most depressed people are probably living in these countries, where there are very few trained **psychiatrists,** and most people cannot afford to buy **antidepressants.** It is estimated that only five percent of depression sufferers in Africa and China get any medical treatment.

HIV and depression

In Uganda, one person in ten is **HIV**-positive, and nearly every family has been affected by HIV and AIDS. Researchers found that 24 percent of Ugandans now suffer from depression—more than four times the highest rate in Western countries. Depressed people often stop caring about themselves. Research shows that many Ugandans have started to do risky things, such as driving very fast and dangerously, or having unprotected sex. Practicing unprotected sex will almost certainly increase the spread of HIV and create a vicious cycle in which depression will become even more widespread.

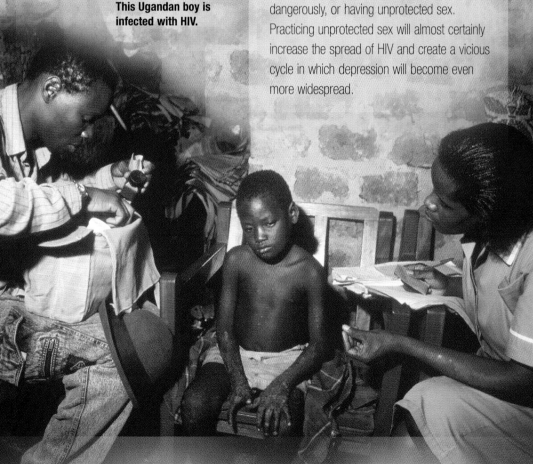

This Ugandan boy is infected with HIV.

15

What Causes Depression?

The fact that depression is described as a "mental" illness can be rather confusing. Depression is very often a **physical** illness, like **diabetes.** While diabetes is caused by a lack of **insulin** in the **pancreas,** depression is usually caused by a low level of mood-related chemicals, called **neurotransmitters,** in the brain. It is the symptoms of depression that are mental, or in the mind.

The three main factors related to depression are physical, **psychological,** and social (to do with the people around us). The root of a person's depression can include more than one of these factors at the same time.

Physical factors

Nearly all depression is linked to a low level of neurotransmitters in the brain. Neurotransmitters pass messages between the brain cells that control our moods. Levels of neurotransmitters can fall for many reasons. This may make people feel terrible, even if everything in their life seems to be going well. It can explain why some people's depression seems to have no obvious cause.

Ongoing problems, such as having constant arguments with a loved one or losing a job, can produce stress chemicals in a person's body. These can lower the level of neurotransmitters in the brain, making a short-term, understandable depression difficult to shake off. Some physical illnesses also affect our levels of neurotransmitters. These illnesses include strokes, Parkinson's disease, and some infectious diseases such as glandular fever.

Seasonal **affective disorder** (SAD) is another type of physical depression. SAD is caused by lack of sunlight during short, dark winter days. Sunlight contains ultraviolet (UV) light. If people do not get enough UV light, their brains may start to produce large amounts of **melatonin**—the same chemical that makes animals such as bears go into hibernation. There are approximately ten million SAD sufferers in the northern United States, but their mood usually improves by springtime, when the days start to get longer.

Alcohol and illegal drugs such as cocaine can also affect a person's brain chemistry, either by causing depression or making it worse. Many depressed people, especially men, use drugs or alcohol to lift their mood for a while. However, they may become **addicted,** needing more of the substance to make them feel better. They may also feel worse each time the effects wear off. Some legal drugs, such as drugs for high blood pressure and arthritis pain relievers, can act as depressants.

Psychological factors

The **psychological** causes of depression may be understandable, such as the death of someone close or a break-up with a boyfriend or girlfriend. Nearly everyone will go through a natural period of grieving or recovery in these situations. However, people who already have a chemical imbalance in their brains may develop major depressive disorder.

People with serious or terminal illnesses, such as cancer or heart disease, often suffer from depression as they come to terms with their illness and face the possibility of death. Depression is also quite common among people suffering from **post-traumatic stress disorder,** a condition that may develop after someone has been attacked or gone through a major disaster such as an earthquake. Post-traumatic depression may not set in until months or even years after a traumatic event.

Post-traumatic depression

In 2002, some British health authorities found it hard to provide enough mental health support to people from war-torn countries (such as Bosnia-Herzegovina) who were trying to settle in the United Kingdom. Even several years after the war had ended, many refugees still suffered from severe post-traumatic depression caused by the stress of trying to survive in a dangerous war zone and seeing many people being killed.

These Bosnian refugees had to leave behind their homes, friends, and belongings. Refugees often have deep mental scars.

Social factors

Scientists believe that some people may learn to be depressed by copying the behavior of people around them. For example, children whose parents are always depressed may grow up thinking it is normal to see everything in a negative light and to expect the worst in every situation. They are sometimes described as the kind of people who always see a glass as being half-empty, rather than half-full.

Some people may develop **cognitive distortions**—fixed, negative ideas. For example, an attractive person may be totally convinced that he or she is ugly or a bad person. If people do well in school, they may think it is because the teacher feels sorry for them, not because they deserved good grades!

"When I get depressed I tend to eat. It's hard to feel good about yourself when you are depressed ... but who has the energy to exercise? I spend so much energy just getting through the day."

(Lisa-Marie, a depressed teenager)

Living in poverty-stricken, slum conditions can make people more likely to suffer from depression.

19

Living with Depression

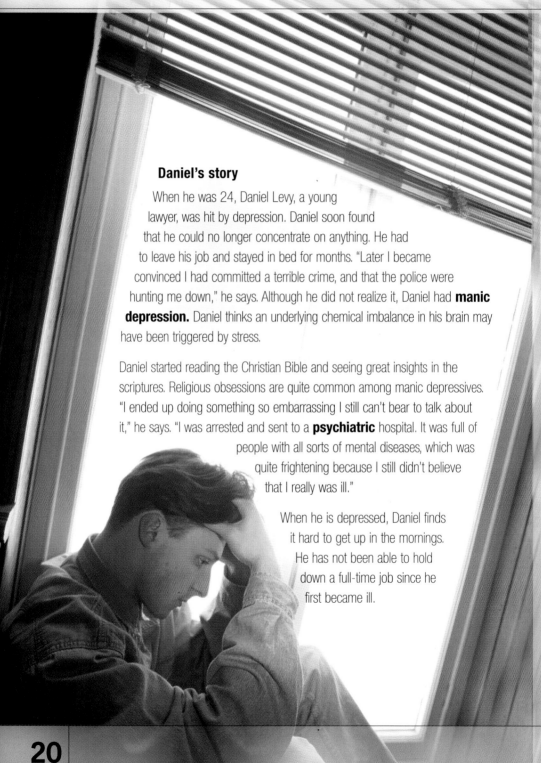

Daniel's story

When he was 24, Daniel Levy, a young lawyer, was hit by depression. Daniel soon found that he could no longer concentrate on anything. He had to leave his job and stayed in bed for months. "Later I became convinced I had committed a terrible crime, and that the police were hunting me down," he says. Although he did not realize it, Daniel had **manic depression.** Daniel thinks an underlying chemical imbalance in his brain may have been triggered by stress.

Daniel started reading the Christian Bible and seeing great insights in the scriptures. Religious obsessions are quite common among manic depressives. "I ended up doing something so embarrassing I still can't bear to talk about it," he says. "I was arrested and sent to a **psychiatric** hospital. It was full of people with all sorts of mental diseases, which was quite frightening because I still didn't believe that I really was ill."

When he is depressed, Daniel finds it hard to get up in the mornings. He has not been able to hold down a full-time job since he first became ill.

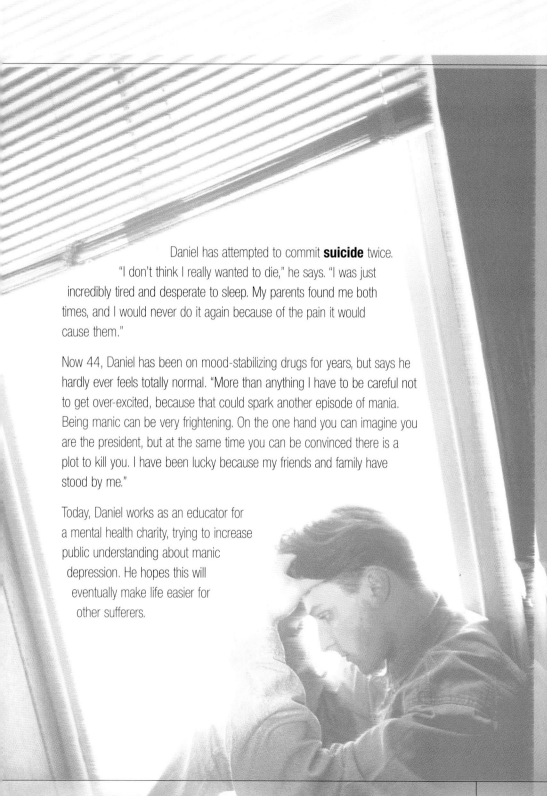

Daniel has attempted to commit **suicide** twice. "I don't think I really wanted to die," he says. "I was just incredibly tired and desperate to sleep. My parents found me both times, and I would never do it again because of the pain it would cause them."

Now 44, Daniel has been on mood-stabilizing drugs for years, but says he hardly ever feels totally normal. "More than anything I have to be careful not to get over-excited, because that could spark another episode of mania. Being manic can be very frightening. On the one hand you can imagine you are the president, but at the same time you can be convinced there is a plot to kill you. I have been lucky because my friends and family have stood by me."

Today, Daniel works as an educator for a mental health charity, trying to increase public understanding about manic depression. He hopes this will eventually make life easier for other sufferers.

The Chemical Brain

Our moods are controlled by very sensitive chemicals in our brains called **neurotransmitters.** Scientists admit that they are far from completely understanding how these chemicals work. However, we do know that depression is often caused when, for some reason, the brain does not produce enough neurotransmitters.

A sense of meaning

The part of the brain where these chemicals affect moods is the frontal lobe. Among other things, the frontal lobe brings together the conscious and unconscious minds to give a feeling of meaning to people's thoughts and emotions. For example, people who have an injury to their frontal lobe often lose the ability to understand the punch lines of jokes and can no longer find the humor funny.

When people are depressed, they often say that life seems to have lost all meaning or pattern. It seems to have become just a chain of pointless events where everything is falling apart. Depression sufferers can no longer find enjoyment in things that used to be fun and mean something to them.

The brain's frontal lobes, involved in controlling our emotions, are shown here in pink.

On the other hand, **manic depressives** going through manic periods—that can last for weeks or months—see great meaning in even the most ordinary events. For them, everything seems perfectly ordered, crystal-clear, and linked together.

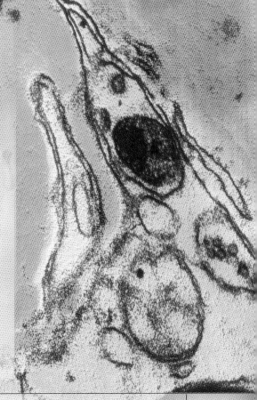

> **"I knew that if anybody spoke to me or looked at me too closely, the tears would fly out of my eyes and the sobs would fly out of my throat and I'd cry for a week. I could feel the tears brimming and sloshing in me like water in a glass that is unsteady and too full."**
>
> (U.S. author Sylvia Plath in her famous novel about depression, *The Bell Jar*)

Defective genes

Scientists at the Royal Ottawa Hospital in Canada have found a faulty **gene** in severely depressed and **suicidal** patients. The gene affects the production of a neurotransmitter, called **serotonin,** in their brains. It is hoped that one day scientists will be able to develop **gene therapy** to remove or repair such defective genes, removing the underlying cause for many people's depression. Another possibility is that they could develop a test to spot faulty genes and identify people most at risk of depression so they can get early treatment.

Hormones and Depression

Some cases of depression seem to be linked to chemicals in our bodies called **hormones.** Hormones control a person's growth and development. Some of the most important ones are the sex hormones **testosterone** and **estrogen.** Men have a fairly constant level of testosterone in their bodies until they grow old. However, a woman's levels of estrogen and other hormones are constantly changing. This may help to explain why, from **puberty** onwards, women seem to suffer from depression more than men.

A woman's hormone levels rise and fall during her monthly **menstrual cycle,** when she is pregnant, and again during **menopause,** which generally happens between the ages of 45 to 55. During menopause, a woman's periods stop completely and the levels of estrogen in her body fall to a fraction of their previous levels. This sudden drop in estrogen levels may cause depression in some women. Many women also feel depressed, emotional, or grouchy just before their period. This is one of the symptoms of **pre-menstrual syndrome (PMS).**

A new baby—cause for joy or depression?

After giving birth, a woman's hormone levels fall quickly. Many people expect a new mother to be full of joy about the new baby. However, in addition to the hormonal changes, a new mother usually feels very tired and is faced with the huge responsibility of looking after a helpless baby. All these factors may add up to make her feel trapped and depressed.

About half of all women suffer from the **baby blues,** which makes them feel quite depressed for a few days after birth. Between five and twenty percent will go on to suffer **postpartum depression,** which normally sets in within a few weeks of the birth. Babies with mothers suffering from postpartum depression may develop more slowly than other babies. They may learn to speak at a later age, have sleep problems, cry more, and smile less often. One or two women in every 1,000 will develop a condition called postpartum **psychosis.** They will suffer from **hallucinations** and **delusions,** and in very severe cases they may end up hurting or even killing themselves or the baby.

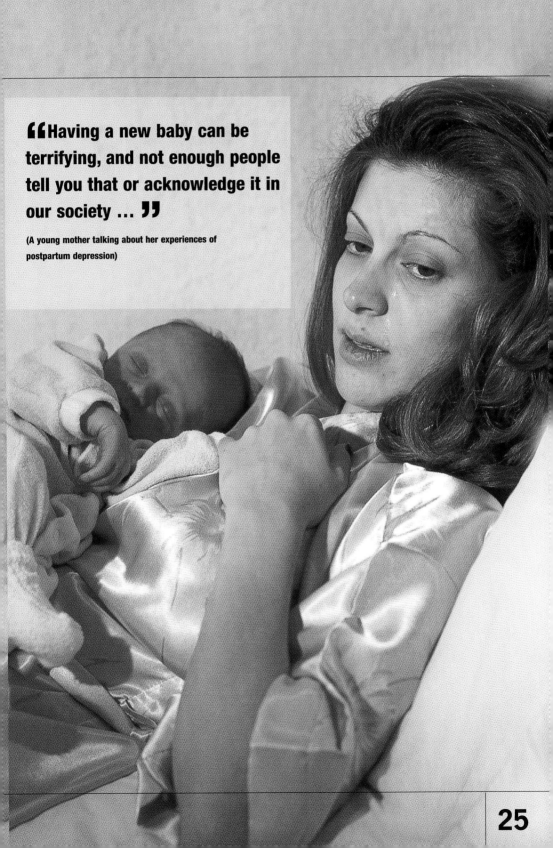

❝Having a new baby can be terrifying, and not enough people tell you that or acknowledge it in our society … ❞

(A young mother talking about her experiences of postpartum depression)

Depression and Genius

People with depression, especially **manic depression,** are often extremely talented and creative. They may be able to use the energy of their illness to achieve fame and fortune or be inspired by their suffering to produce great works of art. Some of the most brilliant actors, artists, politicians, and musicians have been manic depressives. Famous examples include authors Leo Tolstoy and Charles Dickens, composer Ludwig van Beethoven, actor Robert Downey Jr., and musician Sting.

During manic episodes, the levels of **neurotransmitters** in a manic-depressive person's brain shoot up way above normal. This means the sufferer may have huge amounts of energy and need less sleep. During this period, a manic-depressive person might feel intensely happy and confident and take daredevil risks. It is possible to track the mood swings of one manic depressive, the German composer Robert Schumann, by his musical output. He composed nothing at all during 1844, a period of severe depression. However, he wrote an incredible 27 pieces of music during a manic episode in 1849. Today, the mood swings of manic depression can usually be kept under control with drugs, but many sufferers find they miss the highs, when they had boundless energy and felt they could achieve anything.

Comedian Richard Pryor was renowned for making other people laugh, but in his own life he suffered from alcohol and drug abuse and severe depression.

> **❝I was handing in essays that made no sense whatsoever, and because I was manic I thought they were brilliant. I'd receive a grade of 28 percent for an essay that was barely written in sentences and assume it was a typing error.❞**
>
> (Former student Rachael Tooth, talking about her experiences with manic depression while in college)

Misery and art

Many famous people also suffer from **unipolar disorder.** The misery of depression has actually been an inspiration in many cases, such as for the songs of Nirvana's Kurt Cobain and the novels and poems of Sylvia Plath. However, people with unipolar disorder do not usually have such intense periods of energy and output as those with manic depression. They too often find it difficult or impossible to work during a particularly bad bout of depression.

The 19th-century artist Vincent van Gogh cut off his own ear during a bout of severe depression.

Depression and Young People

For many young people, being a teenager feels like being on an emotional roller-coaster ride. Teens can feel angry, miserable, and misunderstood. Parents often laugh this off as "teenage **angst**"—a phase that their children will outgrow. Even expert **psychologists** believed, until recently, that young people could not actually become depressed.

Although depression is probably less common in young people than in adults, the American Academy of Child and Adolescent **Psychiatry** estimates that 3.4 million young people in the United States could be suffering from this condition. **Suicide** figures are one clear piece of evidence of youth depression. In the United States,

about twelve young people kill themselves each day. In many Western countries, the suicide rate has tripled since the 1970s, and only traffic accidents account for more youth deaths.

The diagnosis problem

It is still difficult to know for sure just how common depression is among young people. Often, the illness is not diagnosed correctly. This may be because some doctors still do not believe that young people can suffer from depression. Signs of depression may also be missed because depressed teens tend to behave

Feeling left out or being bullied at school can lead some young people to feel depressed.

very differently from depressed adults and act violent, angry, or rude. Teens themselves may not realize there is anything wrong with them and think it is normal to feel miserable all the time.

People with eating disorders are often also depressed.

Youth depression is often linked to big problems, such as coming from a broken home or being bullied at school. However, television and magazines may also be partly to blame. Teens can be very heavily influenced by the media. On screen, life nearly always seems exciting and full of beautiful people. This can make the reality of a teen's own life seem depressingly dull. In addition, many parents put pressure on their children to do well at school. Children who do not meet these high expectations may feel they have let other people, or themselves, down.

The media link

Scientists at Harvard University found that the eating disorder **anorexia,** which is often linked to depression, became much more common among teenage girls in Fiji after U.S.-style TV programs arrived on the island. Traditionally, dieting was unknown in Fiji and thin women were seen as weak. However, within three years of getting televisions, 74 percent of girls said that they felt "too big" or "fat" and 15 percent were regularly making themselves sick to lose weight.

Why Is Depression on the Rise?

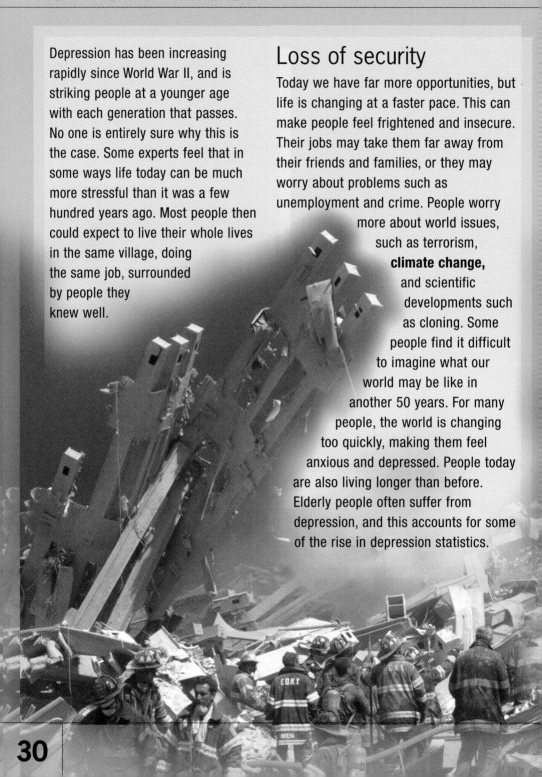

Depression has been increasing rapidly since World War II, and is striking people at a younger age with each generation that passes. No one is entirely sure why this is the case. Some experts feel that in some ways life today can be much more stressful than it was a few hundred years ago. Most people then could expect to live their whole lives in the same village, doing the same job, surrounded by people they knew well.

Loss of security

Today we have far more opportunities, but life is changing at a faster pace. This can make people feel frightened and insecure. Their jobs may take them far away from their friends and families, or they may worry about problems such as unemployment and crime. People worry more about world issues, such as terrorism, **climate change,** and scientific developments such as cloning. Some people find it difficult to imagine what our world may be like in another 50 years. For many people, the world is changing too quickly, making them feel anxious and depressed. People today are also living longer than before. Elderly people often suffer from depression, and this accounts for some of the rise in depression statistics.

Over-diagnosis?

Some experts suggest that the increase in reported depression cases may also be partly due to over-diagnosis. People are slowly learning that depression is curable and is nothing to be ashamed of. This means they are more willing to seek treatment, especially since **antidepressants** are now safer and more effective than ever before. Many of these people are genuinely depressed. However, prescriptions for antidepressants rose by more than 750 percent between 1990 and 2002—much faster than depression rates could have increased. Just as many people think they have the flu when they only have a cold, many people think they are depressed if they just have a temporary attack of the blues.

Most doctors know that many cases of depression go unnoticed. It is therefore possible that some doctors may prescribe antidepressants even if the patient does not match enough symptoms on the checklist. Their patients feel miserable and they want them to feel better. However, this could be dangerous. Antidepressants change the chemistry of the brain, and it is not known what long-term effects this could have for people whose levels of **neurotransmitters** are not actually unbalanced in the first place.

In the weeks and months following the terrorist attacks of September 11, 2001, many people all around the world suffered from shock, **post-traumatic stress disorder,** and depression.

Does Depression Run in Families?

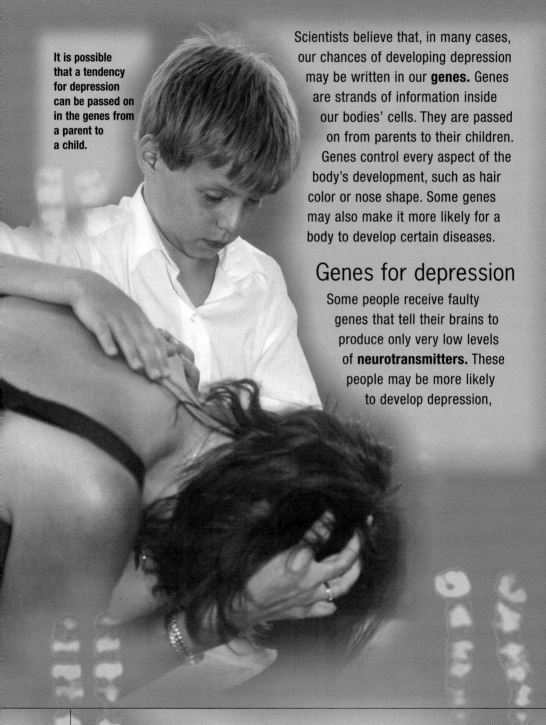

It is possible that a tendency for depression can be passed on in the genes from a parent to a child.

Scientists believe that, in many cases, our chances of developing depression may be written in our **genes.** Genes are strands of information inside our bodies' cells. They are passed on from parents to their children. Genes control every aspect of the body's development, such as hair color or nose shape. Some genes may also make it more likely for a body to develop certain diseases.

Genes for depression

Some people receive faulty genes that tell their brains to produce only very low levels of **neurotransmitters.** These people may be more likely to develop depression, especially if they experience a tough time or emotional problem. There is a strong genetic link for **manic depression,** which on average affects one person in every 100. If a person's parent is a manic depressive, he or she has a one in five chance of developing the illness. If both parents have the condition, the chances increase to one in two. **Unipolar disorder** does not have such a strong genetic link. However, the children of people with depression are still three times more likely to be affected than people in the population at large. However, this may be partly due to the effect of living with depressed parents.

A scientific challenge

An estimated 50,000 genes are thought to be responsible for the development of the brain. It may take many years to identify the specific genes linked to depression. It is important to remember, however, that people are not doomed to suffer from depression, regardless of their genes. They may just be more likely to develop the illness.

Even if a person's identical twin—who has exactly the same genetic make-up—suffers from depression, the risk for the other twin is not 100 percent, but roughly 70 percent. This shows that there are other factors apart from genetics involved in developing depression. A person's way of coping with his or her particular problems has a big impact, too.

Scientists are beginning to unlock the secret information contained in our genes that are found on chromosomes such as these.

Depression and Suicide

An estimated fifteen percent of depression sufferers end up taking their own lives—most often those who have not sought treatment. They just cannot see any end to their misery and feel that **suicide** is the only way to put a stop to their suffering. In 2001, approximately one million people worldwide committed suicide, about one person every 40 seconds. In the United States, more people die from suicide than from murder.

Women are three times more likely than men to attempt to commit suicide. However, men are more likely to succeed. This is because men often use more violent means, such as shooting or hanging themselves. Many women take overdoses of painkillers, and can often be treated in a hospital if found in time.

Some depressed young people take an overdose of pills because they feel angry and want to "make someone sorry." Sadly, many of them cannot be saved in time and die.

The explosion in youth suicide

Youth suicide rates in Western countries have risen rapidly since the 1970s. This is partly because young people, especially young men, are often less likely than adults to get treatment for depression because they may be frightened or embarrassed. People who bottle up their feelings are more likely to end up feeling hopeless and suicidal than people who talk things through with a friend, family member, or counselor.

A cry for help

Parasuicide—in which a person may take an overdose of pills and then call an ambulance, or carry out the act in a place where he or she hopes to be found—is also common among young people. These acts are often cries for help. They are committed by people who do not feel they have any other way to make people pay attention to how bad they are feeling. People who have attempted suicide once will probably feel very depressed and guilty about it and are likely to make another attempt. These people are most likely to repeat a suicide attempt within the first three months, although they may be at risk for several years.

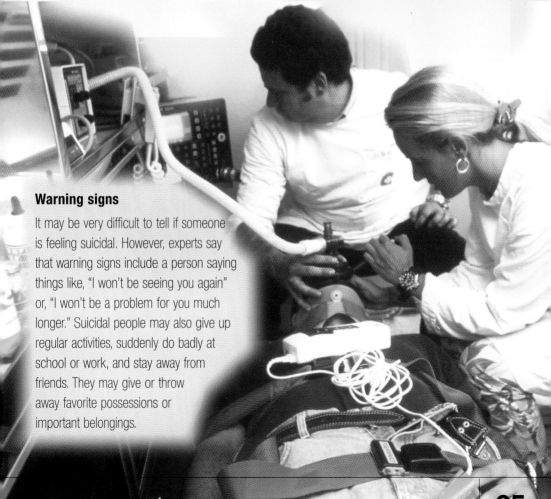

Warning signs

It may be very difficult to tell if someone is feeling suicidal. However, experts say that warning signs include a person saying things like, "I won't be seeing you again" or, "I won't be a problem for you much longer." Suicidal people may also give up regular activities, suddenly do badly at school or work, and stay away from friends. They may give or throw away favorite possessions or important belongings.

Tackling Depression

People with a disease such as scurvy (caused by a lack of vitamin C) will get better if they eat fresh fruit to boost the body's level of vitamin C. In the same way, a person with depression will usually improve by taking medicines called **antidepressants** that restore the balance of **neurotransmitters** in his or her brain. Other treatments are also effective, including counseling or therapies based around art or music.

Fear of treatment

Sadly, however, many people still do not get treatment. They may think that having depression means they are going crazy or that they will be locked away in a **psychiatric** hospital. In fact, people are usually only hospitalized in very severe cases. Many people think that depression is something that happens to other people. They may only visit their doctor when they start to experience **physical** symptoms, such as **insomnia,** weight loss, headaches, or panic attacks.

The mind-body link

It may seem strange that depression, an illness of the mind, can have physical effects like this. However, people's state of mind can have a big effect on their physical health. Depression also lowers sufferers' immune systems, making them more likely to get illnesses such as colds and flu.

People with untreated depression often find it difficult to have a normal life and are more likely to end up homeless, unemployed, **addicted** to alcohol or drugs, or in prison. A child with depression may fail at school and have difficulties getting along with others, always feeling like an outsider.

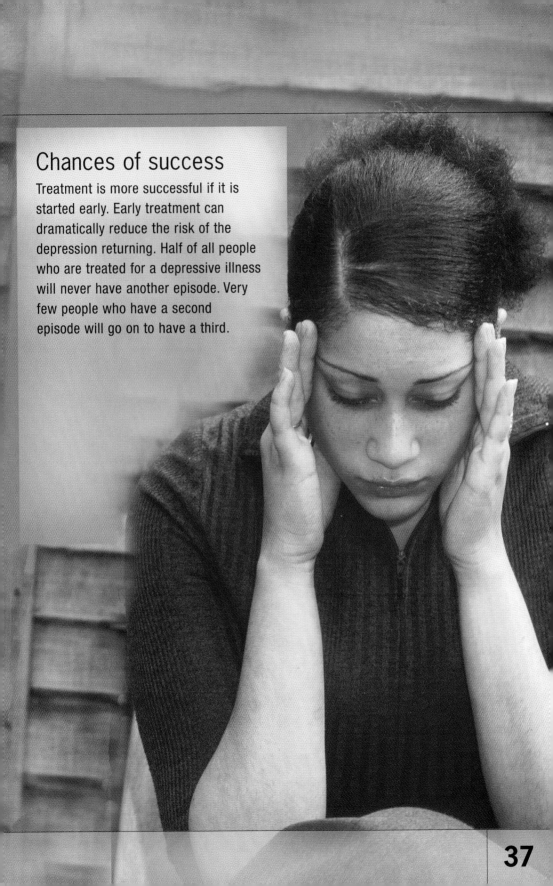

Chances of success

Treatment is more successful if it is started early. Early treatment can dramatically reduce the risk of the depression returning. Half of all people who are treated for a depressive illness will never have another episode. Very few people who have a second episode will go on to have a third.

Plans for the future

To encourage sufferers to get help, governments around the world must educate the public about depression. Sadly, the World Health Organization (WHO) reports that approximately one quarter of the world's countries still have no plans to deal with the illness. The WHO wants governments to make **antidepressants** more widely available and provide public education to remove the embarrassment surrounding depression. It is also calling for better training for doctors to help them recognize the illness in its early stages. Programs dealing with issues linked to depression—such as poverty, unemployment, racism, bullying, and child abuse—are also important.

Progress has already been made in many areas. Since 1991, the American **Psychiatric** Association has run depression screening and information days. So far, more than 100,000 people have been tested for depression. In May 2001, the U.S. Surgeon General set up the country's first **suicide** prevention strategy. Australian authorities launched their first mental health strategy in 1992, and have produced a comic called *Blue Daze* to educate young people about depression. The British government has set up special hot lines for young men in areas of high male unemployment, where depression and suicide rates are rising. Talking through problems is one of the most important first steps in dealing with depression.

For some sufferers, anonymous counseling services can be an important lifeline.

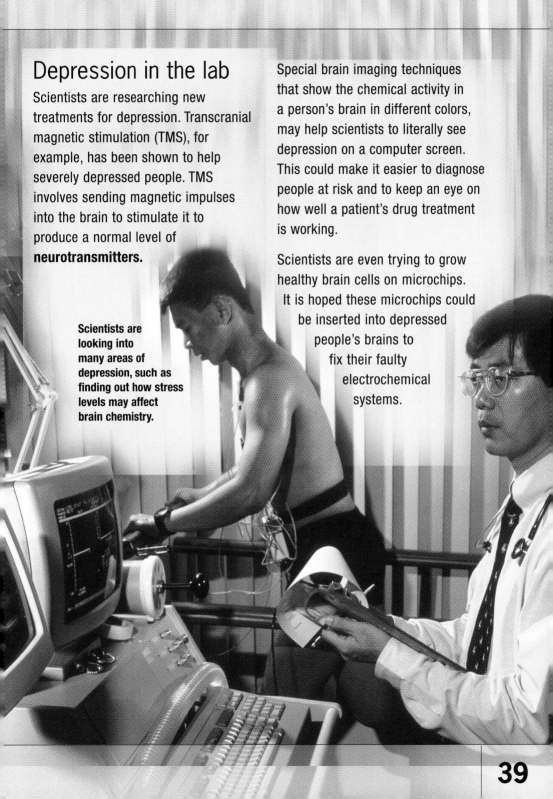

Depression in the lab

Scientists are researching new treatments for depression. Transcranial magnetic stimulation (TMS), for example, has been shown to help severely depressed people. TMS involves sending magnetic impulses into the brain to stimulate it to produce a normal level of **neurotransmitters.**

Special brain imaging techniques that show the chemical activity in a person's brain in different colors, may help scientists to literally see depression on a computer screen. This could make it easier to diagnose people at risk and to keep an eye on how well a patient's drug treatment is working.

Scientists are even trying to grow healthy brain cells on microchips. It is hoped these microchips could be inserted into depressed people's brains to fix their faulty electrochemical systems.

Scientists are looking into many areas of depression, such as finding out how stress levels may affect brain chemistry.

Dealing with depressed friends or relatives

People often do not know how to deal with depressed friends or relatives. They may become frustrated or even angry, and feel that the sufferer is wallowing in self-pity and should be trying harder to be more positive. Well-meaning advice such as, "Pull yourself together," or, "Come on, snap out of it," does not help. If sufferers could just shrug off the depression they would have already done it! Friends and relatives may start to avoid the sufferer, because his or her low mood is draining and brings them down. This can make the sufferer feel even more alone and isolated.

Even though it may seem almost impossible to help or get through to a depressed person, sufferers are often unable to recover alone and depend greatly on the people around them.

Love and support

So how can a depressed person be helped? First of all, the sufferer needs to be told that he or she is loved, no matter what. Many depression sufferers feel that their situation is hopeless. The person may be comforted by being told that he or she is almost definitely going to get better, no matter how bad things seem at the time.

Depressed people should be encouraged to do as much as they can for themselves. However, if it all seems too much for the sufferer, it is helpful to do practical things for them, such as shopping or cleaning. At times, sufferers may even feel too exhausted to get up or bathe themselves.

Sometimes a depressed person needs to get help quickly. Getting help is necessary if a depression sufferer talks much about feeling guilty or wanting to commit **suicide,** or if he or she stops eating or drinking.

People caring for depressed relatives need help, too. It is often a lonely, difficult, and tiring job. Caregivers may sometimes even end up getting depressed themselves, and start to feel it is somehow their fault that the sick person is not getting any better.

It is important that caregivers give themselves a break every now and then. Getting in touch with a local support group can also be a big help. These groups can put people in touch with others going through similar problems.

Legal Matters

Unlike people with **physical** illnesses, people with mental illnesses such as depression can be treated against their will. This happens only in severe cases, such as when doctors think the sufferer is likely to harm himself or herself or someone else. A patient may be sent to a **psychiatric** hospital for a few days or for up to a year. Patients can appeal the doctors' decision, but the process may take several weeks.

Losing a child

A parent with very serious depression may have his or her children taken away and put into foster care if the courts feel the parent cannot care for them properly. Once children have been taken away, it may be difficult for a parent to prove that he or she

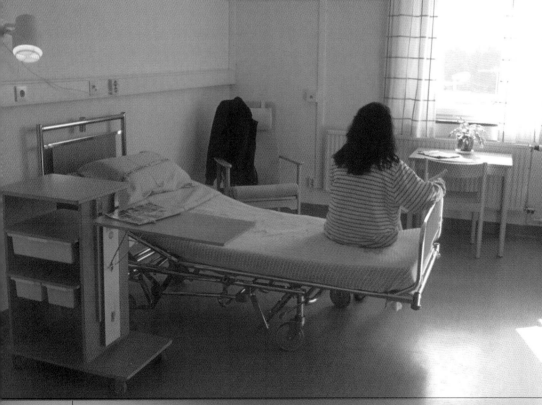

is well enough to care for the children. In making a decision, the court's top concern is the welfare of the child. The feelings of older children may also be taken into account in deciding where they will live.

The cost of care

Another legal issue facing depressed people is medical insurance. Many companies believe that mentally ill people will need costly psychiatric treatment, so they charge them more than usual for the premiums, or they will not provide coverage at all. The U.S. Mental Health Equitable Treatment Act (2001) ruled that health insurance companies should stop doing this. However, some people still find they are being overcharged for the premiums, even if they only suffered from one bout of depression many years ago. This is not the case in countries with free health care, such as the United Kingdom.

Severely ill patients may be placed in a psychiatric ward for some time if doctors feel this is the best way to help them get better.

Discrimination in the workplace

People with depression can face legal problems at work, too. Many employers will not employ depressed people, or may fire them if they find out about their illness. Employers want their businesses to make money and may feel that a depressed person is more likely to take time off. However, a special U.S. government committee has been set up to look into problems in the workplace for people with all kinds of disabilities. In 2000, the committee spent $200,000 creating jobs for people suffering from mental illnesses.

Hiding the illness

In 2002, a survey by the British Mental Health Foundation found that two-thirds of people who have suffered from any kind of mental illness will not tell their employer. Many people said they were frightened they may be fired, would not be promoted, or that fellow workers would find out about the illness and treat them differently.

Treatment and Counseling

Drug treatment

Without treatment, depression usually goes away by itself within about nine months. With **antidepressants,** however, roughly 70 percent of patients get better in as little as three weeks. Women and people with milder depression respond best to this form of treatment.

The human mind is very complex, however, and the reasons for developing and recovering from depression may vary from person to person. This means scientists are still not sure exactly how antidepressants work. Some trials have even shown that the drugs themselves have very little effect, and that people actually cure themselves simply because they believe the drugs will work. Whether they are truly effective or not, antidepressants allow many patients a break from their illness and give them the energy to work out some of their problems. However, it may take a few weeks before a sufferer feels that his or her condition is improving, and the drugs must be taken for several more months after the sufferer feels better. If not, the depression can return even worse than before.

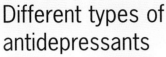

Different types of antidepressants

There are a variety of antidepressants. A person's doctor may advise him or her to try a range of brands until one is found that seems to work best. Antidepressants generally belong to one of three groups: tricyclic antidepressants, selective **serotonin** reuptake inhibitors (SSRIs), and monoamine oxidase inhibitors (MAOIs). They all work to boost or maintain the brain's level of **neurotransmitters.**

The most famous SSRI is Prozac, which is one of the biggest selling drugs of all time. At least 40 million people around the world have taken Prozac since it was introduced in the late 1980s.

Unlike the old-fashioned drugs used for depression 50 years ago, such as pep pills and tranquilizers (which made a person very calm and sleepy), modern antidepressants are not **addictive.** However, some patients can suffer side effects, ranging from stomach bleeding to **insomnia.** This is why it is very important to take antidepressants under the care of a doctor.

Side effects

Tricyclics were first developed in the late 1950s. These early drugs sometimes made people's mouths very dry and gave them blurred vision, but today these side effects are less common. Monoamine oxidase inhibitors (MAOIs) can sometimes react dangerously with foods such as cheese or avocado, causing high blood pressure and heart attacks. For this reason, they are rarely used now, except for people who do not respond to other drugs. Selective **serotonin** reuptake inhibitors (SSRIs) usually do not have dangerous reactions with other medications, are difficult to overdose on, and have fewer side effects than other **antidepressants.** However, they may cause nausea, headaches, diarrhea, and sleeping problems.

Manic depression is usually treated using long-term doses of lithium carbonate, a salt that occurs naturally in small amounts in our food. As a drug, lithium carbonate can help to stabilize a person's moods. It is important to have regular blood tests and drink plenty of water to make sure the level of lithium carbonate in the body is neither too low nor dangerously high. The possible side effects of this treatment may include weight gain and uncontrollable shaking.

Other options

For people with severe depression that does not improve after taking antidepressants, another option is electroconvulsive therapy (ECT). Electric shocks are sent into the brain through special pads attached to the patient's head while he or she is under general anesthetic. No one is quite sure how ECT works, but it does seem helpful. Side effects may include short-term memory loss and aches and pains.

Counseling

Since depression usually has both **physical** and **psychological** causes, the best kind of treatment is often a mixture of drugs and talking therapies. Just talking and being listened to can be a big help to people with depression.

There are many different types of talking therapy and it is important that people find out which method suits them best.

One type of therapy is counseling, in which the depression sufferers can talk through their problems and feelings. During counseling and psychotherapy sessions, sufferers also look into their own pasts to try to understand how and why their depression began.

Counselors help people to get to the root causes of their problems and put them in perspective so they can get on with their lives.

47

Cognitive behavioral therapy (CBT)

Another kind of talking therapy is called cognitive behavioral therapy (CBT). As we have seen, many depressed people have very low self-esteem and a fixed, negative way of thinking, called a **cognitive distortion** that can make people believe they are bad people, boring, or ugly. CBT can help people to reverse their irrational way of thinking. CBT may include relaxation techniques, communication skills, and assertiveness training.

Meditation can be a big help in overcoming depression.

Alternative therapy

Today, alternative medicine is becoming more and more popular. Even though today's **antidepressants** are generally safe and have few side effects, some people do not want to use strong medical drugs to alter their brain's chemistry. They may prefer to use what they see as more natural and gentle treatments. St. John's Wort is a herb that has been shown in some tests to work as well as the antidepressant Prozac. St. John's Wort has become very popular as a natural antidepressant in the past few years. However, it can have some side effects and react dangerously with other medicines.

Studies have been carried out on some other alternative therapies that also seem to have some effect on depression. These include **acupuncture, aromatherapy,** massage, **art therapy** and **music therapy,** and meditation. However, it is not always clear if these therapies really work, or if the sufferers feel better simply because they are taking time to pamper themselves.

Boosts to lift the spirits

Simple things such as listening to music, playing with a pet, taking a walk, taking a hot bath, and eating well can also at least temporarily alleviate the symptoms of depression. Many depressed people do not have the energy to cook properly and they eat only junk food that can make them feel more tired and ill. Exercise, meanwhile, makes the brain release chemicals called **endorphins** that can make people feel happier for a short while.

Seasonal **affective disorder** (SAD) is a type of depression caused in winter by lack of sunlight. The best treatment for this seems to be phototherapy, which involves sitting in front of bright ultraviolet lights.

❝I found that exercise helped. One thing I did was to get straight out of bed and go for a brisk half-hour walk.❞

(Australian actor Garry McDonald, who suffered from panic disorder and depression)

People to Talk To

It may seem very simple, but talking is one of the best ways of dealing with depression. Talking things through can often make it easier to find a way of solving problems or coming to terms with difficult situations. People who keep everything bottled up may become more and more convinced that their situation is hopeless.

Many depression sufferers feel that it is difficult or embarrassing to speak to people who know them, such as parents or friends. There are many professional groups that will listen in confidence to depressed people. Counselors will take the person and his or her feelings and problems seriously. Counselors can often also help in

The Internet can be a means of getting help for a problem without having to speak face-to-face to a real person.

dealing with problems such as studying for exams or making friends at a new school. They also may contact emergency services if they think the sufferer is so depressed that he or she might attempt to commit **suicide.**

Hotlines

Hotlines are usually available 24 hours a day to provide support for people going through a crisis. Since the conversations are anonymous, these services are often used by people who do not feel ready to talk to a doctor, **psychiatrist,** counselor, or therapist.

Help on the web

Many organizations have e-mail counseling services. Teenagers may feel better getting help via the Internet rather than face-to-face. The Samaritans' website, for example, even has a button that can be clicked to make the Samaritans' logo disappear. This means that, in a public place such as an Internet café, no one will realize the person is using a counseling service.

One of the worst things for depressed people is feeling that they are alone. Sharing thoughts and experiences with other people who are in the same situation can be a big help. There are many online chat rooms and discussion boards on all issues that affect teenagers. However, not everyone chatting on a website is as nice as they seem. No one should give out contact details or their address, or arrange to meet anyone from a chat room.

Schools

Many schools have special counselors who are trained to help young people going through various problems, including depression. A trusted teacher can often offer a sympathetic ear or at least give advice about how to find professional help.

Religious leaders

Religious leaders, such as priests, ministers, or rabbis, can help, too. They may be able to give a more spiritual view of a person's problems and how they can be overcome. For some people, religious faith can be very comforting, helping them to see problems as part of a bigger picture and making some kind of sense of their personal difficulties.

Information and Advice

The United States is well served by organizations that provide advice, counseling, and other information relating to depression. All of the contacts listed on this page are helpful springboards for obtaining such advice or for providing confidential information over the telephone or by mail.

Depression contacts

American Psychiatric Association
1400 K Street, NW, Suite 501
Washington, DC 20005
(202) 682-6139
http://www.psych.org

American Psychological Association
750 First Street, NE
Washington, DC 20002
(202) 336-5500
http://www.apa.org

Depression and Bipolar Support Alliance (DBSA)
730 N. Franklin Street, Suite 501
Chicago, IL 60610
(312) 642-0049; (800) 826-3632
http://www.ndmda.org
DBSA educational materials contain useful information about mood disorders in easy-to-understand language. The organization also has a network of groups that provide understanding and support.

National Alliance for the Mentally Ill
200 N. Glebe Road, Suite 1015
Arlington, VA 22203
(703) 524-7600, ext. 7942
http://www.nami.org

National Child Abuse Hotline
(800) 4-A-CHILD or (800) 422-4453
This is a 24-hour counseling service for young people suffering from abuse.

National Institute of Mental Health
5600 Fishers Lane, Room 7-99
Rockville, MD 20857
(301) 443-4536
http://www.nimh.nih.gov

The National Mental Health Association (NMHA)
2001 N. Beauregard Street, 12th Floor
Alexandria, VA 22311
(703) 684-7722; (800) 969-NMHA
http://www.nmha.org
The National Mental Health Association is the oldest and largest nonprofit organization for mental health and illness in the United States. NMHA works to improve the mental health of all Americans through advocacy, education, research, and service.

National Youth Crisis Hotline
(800) HIT-HOME or (800) 448-4663
This service aims to help any young person facing major problems such as drugs, crime, violence, or contemplating suicide.

More Books to Read

Ayer, Eleanor H. *Everything You Need to Know about Depression.* New York: Rosen Publishing Group, Inc., 2001.

Clarke, Julie and Ann Kirby-Payne. *Understanding Weight and Depression.* New York: Rosen Publishing Group, Inc., 2000.

Demetriades, Helen A. *Bipolar Disorder, Depression, and Other Mood Disorders.* Berkeley Heights, N.J.: Enslow Publishers, Inc., 2002.

Jaffe, Steven L. *Prozac and Other Antidepressants.* Broomall, Penn.: Chelsea House Publishers, 1999.

Peacock, Judith. *Bipolar Disorder.* Mankato, Minn.: Capstone Press, Inc., 2000.

Peacock, Judith and Jackie Casey. *Depression.* Mankato, Minn.: Capstone Press, Inc., 2000.

Sommers, Michael A. *Everything You Need to Know about Bipolar Disorder and Manic Depressive Illness.* New York: Rosen Publishing Group, Inc., 2002.

Glossary

acupuncture Chinese alternative therapy that involves inserting fine, steel needles into the skin along energy channels, called meridians

addicted to be dependent on a drug. Drugs that people can become dependent on are *addictive*.

affective disorder another name for depression

angst feelings of anger, fear, and irritability

anorexia eating disorder in which people are obsessed about their weight and starve themselves

antidepressant drug or agent that alleviates symptoms of depression

aromatherapy alternative therapy in which scented essential oils from plants and flowers are massaged into the body

art therapy use of art to allow depressed people to express their feelings and emotions

baby blues mild form of depression, common in women who have just given birth

bipolar disorder another name for manic depression

climate change worldwide change in weather patterns, possibly caused by the gradual warming of the planet by pollution

cognitive distortion fixed, negative idea

Communism political system in which all property is owned by the community and the government restricts personal liberty

delusion false idea or impression. People with delusions may be convinced that someone is following or spying on them.

developing country poor, less industrialized country, such as Ethiopia or India

diabetes disease caused when the body does not produce enough insulin

dysthmia mild form of depression that lasts roughly two years

endorphin chemical released by the brain after an injury or during exercise

estrogen female hormone responsible for a woman's sexual development

gene information within body cells that determines a person's characteristics, such as hair color or nose shape. Genes are passed down to us from our parents.

gene therapy branch of medicine in which doctors may be able to turn off or remove genes that may trigger certain illnesses

hallucination seeing or hearing things that are not really there

HIV Human Immunodeficiency Virus. HIV attacks and destroys the body's immune system.

hormone chemical produced in the body that regulates or stimulates growth and development

insomnia inability to sleep properly

insulin hormone produced in the body to break down sugar

lobotomy operation carried out many years ago on some people with mental illness, in which the frontal lobe of the brain was detached from the rest of the brain

lunatic asylum type of psychiatric hospital used many years ago for people with mental illness

manic depression type of depression marked by alternating moods of elation and misery

meditation technique for calming the mind and reaching inner relaxation, in which people may chant or concentrate on an image or a thought

melancholia sadness or depression

melatonin chemical in the body that has various functions. In large quantities, it causes animals such as bears to go into hibernation during winter.

menopause time when a woman's monthly periods stop, usually between the ages of 45 to 55

menstrual cycle monthly cycle of hormones in a woman's body before menopause

mood disorder another name for depression

music therapy use of singing, listening to music, and imagery to help relieve depression and express feelings and emotions

neurotransmitter chemical that acts as a messenger between the cells of the brain

pancreas gland near the stomach that produces substances to break down food

parasuicide when someone seems to go through the motions of committing suicide, but hopes to be found before they die. It is often seen as a cry for help.

physical having to do with the body

postpartum depression type of depression experienced by up to twenty percent of new mothers. This may be partly due to the level of hormones in their bodies falling very quickly after the birth.

post-traumatic stress disorder
condition of mental stress that sometimes follows a traumatic event

pre-menstrual syndrome (PMS)
condition experienced by many women during the week before their monthly period. It can make them feel grouchy or depressed.

psychiatrist doctor that specializes in treating diseases and problems of the mind. *Psychiatry* is the study of such illnesses.

psychoanalysis type of therapy in which the patient is helped to explore his or her unconscious feelings and to recognize repressed fears and anxieties

psychological having to do with the mind. A person who studies the mind is a *psychologist*.

psychosis severe mental state resulting in hallucinations and irrational behavior

puberty period during which adolescents reach sexual maturity and become capable of reproduction

serotonin important neurotransmitter that can affect moods

sociologist scientist who studies development and change in human society

suicide intentional killing of oneself. A person is *suicidal* if they wish to kill himself or herself.

testosterone male hormone responsible for a man's sexual development

unipolar disorder another name for depression

Index